Pieces of Me
Volume 1

Cecelia Green Jerrell

Published by:
Cecelia Green Jerrell
Bronx, New York

Book Cover: Lakeya Johnson,
Creative Revolution Media

Editing: The Self Publishing Maven,
Robin Devonish Scott

ISBN 13: 978-0990954002

ISBN 10: 0990954005

Bronx, New York

Printed in the United States

Dedication

To my mother,
Ruth Green,
for the courage and strength she passed on—
I'm thankful!

Contents

Beauty of a Sun Setting

Over silent water the sun
is setting

The sky is covered in
rust with streaks of
white

Clouds dark and gray
slide by

The orange and gold ball
slowly slips out of sight

The sun is setting—

beautifully

Inspiration

It's everywhere! It's everything!

Inspiration may strike
at anytime, anyplace,

from anything at all...

an unexpected call, a bouncing ball

an engrossing chore, an egotistical bore

an airplane ride, a blushing bride

a loved one's appreciation, an enemy's
retaliation

an extra special caress while love's
being professed

an ocean's swirling waves as the
morning sun's ablaze

the flavor of favorite candy while
sipping warm brandy

a sniff of fresh fragrance while enjoying
choirs' cadence

However, wherever, when
inspired, I soar

creative juices ignite

thoughts, ideas, words tumble, flow,
rush, and slow

Then, to my delight,

I write!

Night Songs

Dark

Silent

Night

Melodic chirping

Of birds in profusion

makes me think

it

is

a

bright

sunny

morning

Oasis

My

oasis

is

in the desert

It

feels like

I've been here forever

Majestic mountains

surround me, cocoon me

Beckond me

The sizzling sun

makes my happy face

beam

This,

my oasis,

my new home,

suffuses me in

pure bliss

A Pleasure

Early this morning,
I looked out my window
Below, what a delight-
Autumn in full glory a magnificent sight
soaring trees in profusion-
some tall, others not at all
oak, elm,
sycamore,
together
grandly sharing God's space
presenting leaves of pleasing grace
gold, rust, red, green
swaying in gentle breezes
seemingly saying,

"Look till content.
We're here for your pleasure.
Are we not your glorious treasures?"

Las Vegas

Las Vegas
is my dream destination
bright lights,
beautiful, magnificent mountains,
surrealistic sunrises, superb sunsets
ignite my soaring spirits

Las Vegas
is my kind of town
Serenity reigns in my soul
Peace engulfs me
Silence is golden
I am happy

At the Casino

I feel lucky!

How much

will I win?

I feel lucky!

Do you see

my wide grin?

I feel lucky!

Which machine

should I spin?

I lost all my money!

Do you believe gambling is a sin?

A Musical Interlude

High,

Low

with pulsating beats

and

string and bow

the orchestra creates a magical flow

sweetly the chorus sings

song after song

voices so in harmony

swaying the audience

to wonderment

igniting and delighting

music lovers' appreciative senses

Serenity

yellow, pink, red

fragrant flowers flourish

in blazing glory

as soft, gentle breezes whisper close to
my ear

light and dark green

leaves

adorning stately trees

rustle in the wind

through the shadows,

a winding, narrow path

leads

straight

to

my

old,

cozy

home

Unwind

Let it all hang out

Unwind

Do your thing

Unwind

Take it easy

Unwind

Lighten up

Unwind

Loosen up

Unwind

Be free

Unwind

Unwind

Unwind

Relax

Then,

Recharge

Return revived, renewed, and reinvigorated

At the Beach

umbrellas bright and cheery

give needed shade

kites silently color the air

beach towels dot the sand

sailboats swiftly glide by

birds coo noisily

now and then helicopters and airplanes
almost disturb the peace

at the beach

sunbathers read parallel

swimmers enjoy the water's wonderful
waves

others lounge, stretch or sleep

beachcombers seek the perfect shell

parasailers fly high in the clear sky

refreshing breezes touch the skin

laughing children play and dig

no one is talking on a cell

a cool dip in the ocean blue

is just right for me and you

Isn't life just grand at the beach?

Retirement Whirl

I have a problem getting up in the
morning

so often during the day, you'll catch me
yawning

At the UFT Retiree Center, friends and I
love to mingle

as we talk, Salsa and sing a jingle

Discussing short stories and writing
memoirs and poems

are what make me leave my comfy
home

I spend lots of time taking these
rewarding classes

while wearing sneakers and red reading
glasses

Anytime is a good time to crochet or
knit

as long as I get to laugh, eat and sit

If you ask: What is your favorite passion?

I'd certainly answer: Enjoying the latest
fashion

In the lounge, I munch delicious chips

right before embarking on exciting trips

A tour of Gracie Mansion and tea in the
Blue Room

ward off any chance of boredom that
may dare to loom

It's take the bus to the theater at 5:15

Where I'll sit in the mezzanine

Many days are spent doing colorful
beading

And then at night, I wind down reading

So, as you can see, there's no time for
cleaning—

Only for what gives retirement meaning

Just Do It

Just do it

is what I tell myself so many times a say

Just do it

is what I think to myself while enjoying
the sun's rays

Just do it

is what I hear in my mind as I gaze at the
sparkling bay

Just do it

is what I ponder as on the grass I lay

Just do it

is what I feel in my heart when in the
midst of a fray

Just do it

is what means so much when I am
down and gray

Just do it

is what I heard as the answer when I sat
down to pray

Just do it

is what I finally did when You revealed
the best way

Just did it

is now what I can triumphantly say

Ever Too Late?

Is it ever too late to follow your dream?

Is it ever too late to want something so much you can taste it?

Is it ever too late to wish for something you've never had?

Is it ever too late to desire something of your own?

Is it ever too late to hope for what will make you happy?

Is it ever too late to take the bull by the horns and discover, pursue, persist, endeavor, seek, strive and continue until you can see the light near the end of the tunnel?

NO!

IT IS NEVER TOO LATE!

One can always

HOPE

TRUST

EXPECT

BELIEVE

PLAN, PURSUE, PERSEVERE

ACHIEVE

THRIVE

FLOURISH

I'm Still Learning

I'm still learning

Wow,

I'm having so much fun

I'm still earning certificates by the ton

I'm still burning for wisdom and
knowledge

That's why I'm still attending college

I'm still churning to experience life's
many pleasures

I'm still yearning to discover my treasures

I'm still turning page after page
searching for connections

I'm still finding my way through a maze
of contradictions

Knowledge won't elude me

For I'm seizing opportunities

to expand my mind and possibilities

I'm still pursuing life's tough questions

Yes, I'm still learning

Though my head may be spinning

I'm focused, committed and contented

For, I'm still learning

Health

I'm trying to greatly improve my health
for my body is my greatest wealth

Most times, I know I'm progressing
though, sometimes I know I'm stressing

I'm trying to shrink my stomach and
thighs while increasing my memory and
the acuity of my eyes

I've cut out French fries and delicious
apple pies

No more candy, pizza and soda, I
exercise to a strict quota

I consume nutritious food I need, discuss
engrossing books I read

Drink plenty of water, laugh with my
darling daughter

Sleep eight hours a night so I can feel
somewhat bright

I'm rejuvenated, reenergized, hot

I remember what's important

I let go of what's not

My health is my wealth

Spring

Spring,

a time for me to start anew

To cast out the old and herald in the new

I must be bold to get my due

If truth be told, I don't want your view

Keep your opinions on hold, for I don't want to rue

I'm aiming for the gold while following my own rules

Spring forward I will with my own agenda

to spark this

long awaited adventure

All By Myself

All by myself,

I am beginning my journey

All by myself

I am looking forward to being more,

seeing more, doing more,

to feeling every bit of enjoyment I can

All by myself

I will search for experiences to foster

a newness of spirit,

a reawakening of power, courage, and
a sense of wonder

All by myself, I will

All by myself, I will

All by myself, I will

From Problem to Beautiful

Before

Tough, rough, gray, and frayed

Spiky, wiry, untidy and tangled

Drab, dull, twisted, and bristly

Frizzed, frazzled, fuzzy and thin

Now

Smooth, soft, shiny, and strong

Bright, brown, glowing, and luxuriant

Thick, tidy, healthy, and growing

Stylish, groomed, dyed,

but natural

Forever…

CONTENT

I Am

Look at me!

Check me out!

Am I looking good?

Am I put together?

Do I have it going on?

Looking stylish, am I?

Yes!

I know I'm rocking this look!

I'm bold,

fashion-forward

fabulous, fit!

I am sizzling, soaring, spicy,

quite a hit!

Feel my heat!

I'm bright, electrifying

making heads turn, making a huge flash

I'm rocking this runway,

rocking this world!

I'm rocking this number,

this runway,

your world!!!

Chic, chic, chic, I am

It's a Pretty Party

It's a pretty party
And...
...you're not invited
don't even show your face
don't knock on my door
don't ring my bell
don't try to plead your case

You won't get to first base
You just can't come in
This party is for the "in" crowd
the posh, the beautiful, the wild
We'll be bold, brassy, loud
getting our party on
swaying to the beat
feeling the heat
certainly not staying in our seats

It's a pretty party
We 're going to party hardy
We'll eat, drink, dance
Looking cool and debonaire
As we exude our individual flair

But, I Think

You think I'm white-haired, ancient, old

But, I think hey, I can still fold

You think, I'm heavy with the weight of
years

But, I think boy that's no reason for fears

You think I'm over the hill

But, I think are you kidding I never spill

You think I am archaic and time worn

But, I think really have you heard me
blow my horn?

You think I've lost my faculties

But, I think just try putting me in a facility

You think I have one foot in the grave

But, I think wow how did I get to be so
brave?

You think I'm at an extremely advanced
age

But, I think sonny this is not my last page

You think I'm well past my prime

But, I know I have plenty of time

because

I still believe

I'm a spring chicken

Make Yourself at Home

Embark on a Journey

Dream of Love

Dance and Sing

every morn

Believe in Hope

Live in Love

LAUGH, LAUGH, LAUGH

Cry

Pray

Shout,

"Thank You,"

every eve

For a journey unending

Embrace life—

Make yourself at Home in Your

Own Life

Danced in the Spotlight

So happy, so very, very thrilled
My body could not, would not still
I was energized and motorized
My feet danced a drill
Jumped up, caught up in my zeal
Moved to the left with skill
Shimmied right, knew my will

I danced in the spotlight
Feeling really bright
I'm a sensational sight
Having a fabulous night—
Because…
I danced in the spotlight
Yes, I danced in the spotlight

If I Could Sing

If I could beautifully sing
To you, joy I would gladly bring
You would hear my southern accent
And certainly feel so content
To you, joy I would gladly bring

As I'd huskily sing and sing
You would no doubt feel like a king
Knowing you were heavenly sent
If I could beautifully sing

If you'd flash an engagement ring
I would hardly believe this thing
Taking place in a little tent
This would be a thrilling event
You'd hear me sing a ding a ling
If I could beautifully sing

I Feel Like Dancing

Come on
Put on your comfy shoes
Don't be a boor
Join me on the dance floor
I feel like dancing
I gyrate to the fierce beat
body ready for this feat
sashaying to the west
shaking with mighty zest
it's fun, great, so right
I'm a sensational sight
I am dancing, I am dancing
Clapping, snapping, stomping, too
Twisting, turning, doing the Boogaloo
Swirling, twirling, dipping deep
Hope you're watching my fancy feet
I am dancing to my own beat
Come on join me—
There's always room for one more
on the dance floor

I Know

I know I'm not crazy
but all around me
Insanity is what I hear and see—
makes me want to pick up, take off,
flee
The absurdity of it all
Induces me to hang my head and bawl
I know I'm not crazy
So I retreat to a wailing wall and
wrap myself in a prayer shawl
I stand in need of comfort,
I yearn for relief,
Certainly I'll be triumphant
I'll find true peace
The madness around me has to wither
and cease
For,
I know I'm not crazy, not me

Lifesavers

They are lifesavers, it is true
That is why we follow the rules
When we do not, many suffer
And lives are very much rougher

Making changes we must attend to
Focus on right and follow through
So you will not need a buffer
They are lifesavers, it is true

Now that you have made a break
through
I must applaud your point of view
Your ways no longer bring wonder
You have become so much tougher
Laws are for everyone
They are lifesavers, it is true

Laughter

You make us laugh, you do

Especially when seeing your tie askew

Giggles and snickers we make in glee

As amusement galore you guarantee

When you dribble your coconut stew

The others who compete, try to outdo you

But do not have your wacky point of view

Their jokes make us think of smelly debris

You make us laugh, you do

Your silly antics I performed in Timbuktu

But the savvy audience cried, "Boo! Boo!"

They'd seen you juggling purple potpourri

Knew you were a clown of the tenth degree

Screamed out, "You're the best! Thank you!"

You make us laugh, you do

Tricky

You schemed and finagled

Swindled and plundered

Your chicanery knew no bounds

Your con game was on

I couldn't stand my ground

You're an imposter, a cheat, a fraud

The façade of innocence

You did portray

Was really wickedness on display

I was a fool, didn't know you'd be cruel

I believed but your plan was to deceive

You're a menace, a shyster, a fake

Thought I would break

But, I'm calling your bluff

For, I am tough

No longer deluded or secluded

I'm keen, capable, strong

You'd better watch out

Because there's no doubt

You did me wrong and

I'm singing a get revenge song

Currency

Banks keep it
we deposit it
withdraw it
and budget it

spend it
on baubles and bills
until our salaries
stretch no longer

necessary controls
cutting expenses
may save
us

If we can invest in
stocks and bonds
will we be sheltered?
Decisions, decisions

When the Fun Stops

When the fun stops

Your money is gone

Joy ends

Your head spins

You know pain

There's no gain

You didn't win

Certainly no flashing grin

You are ready to drop

Because the fun really did stop

The machines are cold

You acquired no gold

No fun

No fun

No fun

Our Gems

Steadfastly standing

mountains

woo our attention

day after day after day

These massive jewels

always merit mentioning,

would not you agree?

Memorializing

the grandiosity of

our timeless treasures

feels so right

to me

A Kiss Forever

I savor your kiss
Dear, oh, light of my life, this
warmth and affection
seal our connection

An amorous caress
tenderly attests to love
everlasting

We kiss, a gentle kiss-
I hear a melody
as we embrace endlessly
in pure paradise-
a forever kiss
kiss
kiss

Gossip

Heard a rumor
Tell me it's not true
don't want to believe
you tittle tattled what
I confidentially told you

Heard a rumor
Tell me it's not true
Did you share
all the innermost secrets
I confidentially told you?

Heard a rumor
Tell me it's not true
Did you circulate
the private notions
I confidentially told you?

Heard a rumor
Turned out to be true
You prattled my business
No longer are you
my confidant,
my friend

A Winning Wink

Did I see you wink
at me as you passed the rink
carrying your drink?

Let me really think
of the kind of earnest link
we should perhaps sink .

Promise me a mink
believe you me,

back I will blink

Hushed

Slowly your head sinks

The pillow warm, fluffed

You snooze

Cozy, drowsy

In the land of nod

You snore

I cradle you

Content, I drift off,

too

Alone

in the middle of nowhere

staring unseeingly

silence,

tasting the bitterness of betrayal

Touching bottom,

isolated,

out in the cold

Closing my eyes,

I go deep inside,

taking deep, deep breaths

filling with fresh air,

reviving air

Opening my eyes,

I concede seclusion,

I acknowledge tranquility, comfort

I identify survival

I'm alive, again

❧ 50 ☙

Absurd 58

Peculiarly prudish, penny-pinching

pairs of pretty paramours

purchased plenty of passable
pocketbooks

packed with pickles, pies and plums

pressed parallel to parachutes, palms
and purple pacifiers

for pampering pious pedestrians

pretending to proclaim pure perfection

in perfectly painting pale palaces,
pumpkins and peaches

for puny punks punching purchasable
puzzles

punishable by pure-blooded pundits

performing in protective parades

provoked by prying, pubescent
publicists

preparing purposeless pursuits

preventing previous pals from

procuring perplexing pledges

Lighten up

Cool down

No need to defend your position

I'm not a magician tricking you into
submission

You exhibit too much suspicion

for a person in your condition

Use your powerful volition

to display self-possession

I'm no trickster, deceiver, cheat

wouldn't jeopardize our connection
that is divine

just trying to strategize,

predict my next action to keep us
entwined-

strengthening our commitment is my
intention

Ultimately,

what is your true mission?

www.ingramcontent.com/pod-product-compliance
Lightning Source LLC
Chambersburg PA
CBHW071640040426
42452CB00009B/1707